ROYAL
BOTANIC
GARDENS
KEW

DESK DIARY
1998

STUDIO
DESIGNS

AN IMPRINT OF EBURY PRESS

PERSONAL DETAILS

NAME

....

ADDRESS

....

....

TELEPHONE (HOME)   (BUSINESS)

....

FIRST PUBLISHED IN 1997 BY STUDIO DESIGNS
AN IMPRINT OF EBURY PRESS, RANDOM HOUSE UK LIMITED,
RANDOM HOUSE, 20 VAUXHALL BRIDGE ROAD,
LONDON SW1V 2SA

RANDOM HOUSE UK LIMITED REG. NO. 954009

SET IN TRAJAN AND BEMBO

DESIGNED BY NIGEL PARTRIDGE

PRINTED AND BOUND IN SINGAPORE

ISBN 0 09 185274 9

FRONT COVER: *Gentiana acaulis (G. excisa)*
From the top of the Grammont, Mentone, 29th April 1897

TITLE PAGE: *Viola* SP.
Mentone, 25th March 1896

1998 YEAR PLANNER

JANUARY
M	T	W	T	F	S	S
			1	2	3	4
5	6	7	8	9	10	11
12	13	14	15	16	17	18
19	20	21	22	23	24	25
26	27	28	29	30	31	

FEBRUARY
M	T	W	T	F	S	S
						1
2	3	4	5	6	7	8
9	10	11	12	13	14	15
16	17	18	19	20	21	22
23	24	25	26	27	28	

MARCH
M	T	W	T	F	S	S
30	31					1
2	3	4	5	6	7	8
9	10	11	12	13	14	15
16	17	18	19	20	21	22
23	24	25	26	27	28	29

APRIL
M	T	W	T	F	S	S
		1	2	3	4	5
6	7	8	9	10	11	12
13	14	15	16	17	18	19
20	21	22	23	24	25	26
27	28	29	30			

MAY
M	T	W	T	F	S	S
				1	2	3
4	5	6	7	8	9	10
11	12	13	14	15	16	17
18	19	20	21	22	23	24
25	26	27	28	29	30	31

JUNE
M	T	W	T	F	S	S
1	2	3	4	5	6	7
8	9	10	11	12	13	14
15	16	17	18	19	20	21
22	23	24	25	26	27	28
29	30					

JULY
M	T	W	T	F	S	S
		1	2	3	4	5
6	7	8	9	10	11	12
13	14	15	16	17	18	19
20	21	22	23	24	25	26
27	28	29	30	31		

AUGUST
M	T	W	T	F	S	S
31					1	2
3	4	5	6	7	8	9
10	11	12	13	14	15	16
17	18	19	20	21	22	23
24	25	26	27	28	29	30

SEPTEMBER
M	T	W	T	F	S	S
	1	2	3	4	5	6
7	8	9	10	11	12	13
14	15	16	17	18	19	20
21	22	23	24	25	26	27
28	29	30				

OCTOBER
M	T	W	T	F	S	S
			1	2	3	4
5	6	7	8	9	10	11
12	13	14	15	16	17	18
19	20	21	22	23	24	25
26	27	28	29	30	31	

NOVEMBER
M	T	W	T	F	S	S
30						1
2	3	4	5	6	7	8
9	10	11	12	13	14	15
16	17	18	19	20	21	22
23	24	25	26	27	28	29

DECEMBER
M	T	W	T	F	S	S
	1	2	3	4	5	6
7	8	9	10	11	12	13
14	15	16	17	18	19	20
21	22	23	24	25	26	27
28	29	30	31			

1999 YEAR PLANNER

JANUARY
M	T	W	T	F	S	S
				1	2	3
4	5	6	7	8	9	10
11	12	13	14	15	16	17
18	19	20	21	22	23	24
25	26	27	28	29	30	31

FEBRUARY
M	T	W	T	F	S	S
1	2	3	4	5	6	7
8	9	10	11	12	13	14
15	16	17	18	19	20	21
22	23	24	25	26	27	28

MARCH
M	T	W	T	F	S	S
1	2	3	4	5	6	7
8	9	10	11	12	13	14
15	16	17	18	19	20	21
22	23	24	25	26	27	28
29	30	31				

APRIL
M	T	W	T	F	S	S
			1	2	3	4
5	6	7	8	9	10	11
12	13	14	15	16	17	18
19	20	21	22	23	24	25
26	27	28	29	30		

MAY
M	T	W	T	F	S	S
31					1	2
3	4	5	6	7	8	9
10	11	12	13	14	15	16
17	18	19	20	21	22	23
24	25	26	27	28	29	30

JUNE
M	T	W	T	F	S	S
	1	2	3	4	5	6
7	8	9	10	11	12	13
14	15	16	17	18	19	20
21	22	23	24	25	26	27
28	29	30				

JULY
M	T	W	T	F	S	S
			1	2	3	4
5	6	7	8	9	10	11
12	13	14	15	16	17	18
19	20	21	22	23	24	25
26	27	28	29	30	31	

AUGUST
M	T	W	T	F	S	S
30	31					1
2	3	4	5	6	7	8
9	10	11	12	13	14	15
16	17	18	19	20	21	22
23	24	25	26	27	28	29

SEPTEMBER
M	T	W	T	F	S	S
		1	2	3	4	5
6	7	8	9	10	11	12
13	14	15	16	17	18	19
20	21	22	23	24	25	26
27	28	29	30			

OCTOBER
M	T	W	T	F	S	S
				1	2	3
4	5	6	7	8	9	10
11	12	13	14	15	16	17
18	19	20	21	22	23	24
25	26	27	28	29	30	31

NOVEMBER
M	T	W	T	F	S	S
1	2	3	4	5	6	7
8	9	10	11	12	13	14
15	16	17	18	19	20	21
22	23	24	25	26	27	28
29	30					

DECEMBER
M	T	W	T	F	S	S
	1	2	3	4	5	6
7	8	9	10	11	12	13
14	15	16	17	18	19	20
20	21	22	23	24	25	26
27	28	29	30	31		

HISTORY OF KEW, ITS LIBRARY AND ARCHIVES

The Royal Botanic Gardens, Kew, is situated less than ten miles from Central London on the banks of the River Thames, and comprises more than 300 acres containing over 35,000 species of plants. It is best known as the foremost authority in the world on the conservation of plants and, of course, as one of the most famous gardens in Britain, seen by a million visitors every year.

It consists mainly of two estates which originally belonged to the Royal family. In 1759, Augusta, Dowager Princess of Wales and mother of George III, laid out 9 acres of her estate as a botanic garden. William Aiton became her head gardener, Lord Bute her botanical adviser and Sir William Chambers, the architect, designed a number of buildings for the garden and surrounding pleasure grounds.

George III later joined his grandfather's neighbouring Richmond estate with that of Kew and Sir Joseph Banks became the unofficial director. Banks sent collectors all over the world in pursuit of plants of economic, scientific or horticultural interest, and employed Francis Bauer as Botanical artist at Kew.

Sir William Hooker was, at the time, illustrating and directing Curtis's Botanical Magazine, and together with Walter Hood Fitch, one of the most accomplished and prolific botanical illustrators, continued the fine tradition of botanical illustration at Kew.

In 1840 the botanic garden was handed over to the State, and in the following year Sir William Hooker was appointed as the first official director. He established both the Herbarium and Library in 1852.

Botanical illustration is still used today as the most accurate and detailed way of portraying plants from the scientific as well as an artistic viewpoint. The Library and Archives at Kew holds thousands of original illustrations and paintings, and since 1852 many fine paintings and engravings have been donated to enhance Kew's scientific resources.

THE MRS FORSTER
COLLECTION

The illustrations contained in this year's diary have been taken from the Sidney E Forster collection which was recently re-discovered in Kew's archives.

Although very little is known about Mrs Forster, we do know that she flourished in the 1890s. The collection was given to Kew in 1934 by Miss Alice Pepys, her niece, who correctly thought that the collection would be of botanical interest to Kew scientists. It has remained in the Archives, almost untouched, until today.

Mrs Forster's paintings embody a synergy between flower painting and botanical illustration in that whilst they display enormous attention to detail and scientific accuracy, her paintings are also delicately beautiful.

This unique collection of illustrations was painted on identically sized cards and meticulously arranged in leather-bound boxes, each one with its own index of contents. Mrs Forster was careful to arrange the paintings in botanical order of plant families. The collection itself reveals a marvellous glimpse into this Edwardian's lady's travels, dedication and life.

There are six boxes in all, illustrating the indigenous wildflowers of the French Riviera and the Alps. The illustrations in the 1998 diaries have been taken from the Riviera collection.

Derwentwater from Castle Head.

DEC 1997 – JANUARY 1998

29 MONDAY WEEK 1

Count the year by memories
that bring happiness to you
Good friends you've known
Good times you've had
The dreams you've seen come true.

30 TUESDAY

Artist at St Ives. – John Ambrose

SETÚBAL   CHAPEL BUILT 1490
ARRABIDA STONE

GORDON NAPIER
VIC DAMONE

31 WEDNESDAY
FIRST DAY OF RAMADAN

ÓBIDOS
ALCOBAÇA
SALIR – DO – PORTO

0845 6387

Anne Baxter Celeste Holm –

Susie Voltaire

1 THURSDAY
HOLIDAY, NEW YEAR'S DAY

National Institute of Carpet & Floor Layers
4d St Mary's Place The Lace Market Nottm
NG1 1PH (0115 958 3077)

Ramsden & Carr

Jelly Tots   Pickhalating

Mrs Barbara Tannerhill

JANUARY

*#06#

2 FRIDAY
HOLIDAY, SCOTLAND (TBC)

Lawnmower   9 254 030

JRA

Kitchen light. Crompton
       T8 White   3500°K   58W
Halophosphate Fluorescent lamp

3 SATURDAY

Tuesday night   Wednesday night   Thursday night
Mrs Lemon Sole   Pork casserole   Chicken Konigzt
Watercress   Trifle   Rice pudding   Sponge pudding
    Sauce

Amethyst for devotion.   Robert Andrew Mark

4 SUNDAY

There's no point in being modest
when everyone knows how good you are

George Roys Lias
                                    Laudlum
Eaglesham   ... Opium & Alcohol

| DECEMBER 1997 | | | | | | | JANUARY 1998 | | | | | | | FEBRUARY | | | | | | |
M	T	W	T	F	S	S	M	T	W	T	F	S	S	M	T	W	T	F	S	S
1	2	3	4	5	6	7				1	2	3	4							1
8	9	10	11	12	13	14	5	6	7	8	9	10	11	2	3	4	5	6	7	8
15	16	17	18	19	20	21	12	13	14	15	16	17	18	9	10	11	12	13	14	15
22	23	24	25	26	27	28	19	20	21	22	23	24	25	16	17	18	19	20	21	22
29	30	31					26	27	28	29	30	31		23	24	25	26	27	28	

9291702

NOTES

Have you asked your Ins Co if you are
fully covered for the claim

After reading th studying my Deeds
is it your opinion that a third party
Re 118 Thoresby Dear Miss Bagga. should be involved.

        I must point out that
Mr Duncan Newbutt the Environmental Health
Officer says that because the fault in the drain
pipe is between myself no 33 Brookside Ave
& no 42 Brookside — we are the two
householders who should pay. He says that
because part of the drain passing through the
garden of no 118 Thoresby Rd ~~& out into the
sewer on Thoresby Rd~~ isn't affected by
the present problem that Householder ~~should not~~ cannot be
called upon to contribute to the cost of
repair. He said ~~that~~ categorically that-That
is the law. quite There must be a solicitor
in your practice who is familiar with the
law regarding underground drains & sewers.
Is it your opinion

17 SATURDAY

Peter Featherstone...

9258717. ...1.26...

Colin.

Michael Th Carrick

18 SUNDAY

Strapleford Park

Nith of the North rejoice   *1931   4*
                                    1938   7

In the bleak midwinter

3rd Floor

Smallbrook

Queens Way Birmingham

B 5 4HA

ANEMONE HORTENSIS
Gathered in the Gorbio Valley, Mentone, 10th March 1876

6.53.

0800028508

20 TUESDAY ◐

Joshua Bell · North Rd

Walbrook Cl

Tilbury Rise

9291702

02082994327

Sir Thomas Allen

THE BAR IS

21 WEDNESDAY

Gravetye Manor

Bill Maynard

Cowan

Copestake

22 THURSDAY

Nick Munro

N O T E S

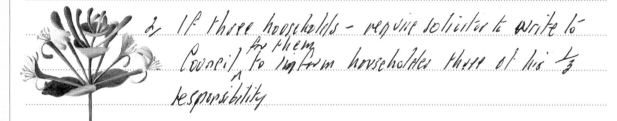

1. Solicitor will give decision as to whether two households or three are responsible for upkeep of drain

2. If three households - require solicitor to write to Council, for them to inform householder three of his ⅓ responsibility

3. Find a man to dig hole (perhaps for cash) to ascertain depth of problem and, after inspection by Council, remedy.

4. If three, or only two, householder insurances will cover all costs then it would be easier to let Council do work but this will be far more expensive than a private contractor.

5. If it proves necessary complain to Insurance Cº that their legal cover was no use and that you have had to pay for your own legal advice and what do they propose to do about it.

Insurance Co may argue it is Mr Rowe's responsibility

JANUARY

5 MONDAY ◗   *The Oakhouse Restaurant Stamford*

6 TUESDAY
EPIPHANY HOLIDAY. ITALY   Bamboo stand Bamboo plant stand
Four pictures (prints) Langley pottery Teapot Hot water jug
with jug sugar basin Two vases.

7 WEDNESDAY   NESS GARDENS.
GERANIUM MADERENSE
TREE WITH RED BARK & STRIPES ROUND
PRUNUS SERRULA ROSACEAE (W. CHINA)

8 THURSDAY   Gwen Francom Davis

JANUARY

9 FRIDAY   Would they replace unit if faulty

Now much per year.   8599267 : Mr Green.

35
77
60

10 SATURDAY   Tomb of the unknown warrior in

Westminster Abbey.

"Sleep on, thy mighty dead;

A glorious tomb. they've found thee!"

11 SUNDAY

Wishing you a Birthday as pleasant as possible

Bordertoo Ladys Comfortes

DECEMBER 1997						
M	T	W	T	F	S	S
1	2	3	4	5	6	7
8	9	10	11	12	13	14
15	16	17	18	19	20	21
22	23	24	25	26	27	28
29	30	31				

JANUARY 1998						
M	T	W	T	F	S	S
			1	2	3	4
5	6	7	8	9	10	11
12	13	14	15	16	17	18
19	20	21	22	23	24	25
26	27	28	29	30	31	

FEBRUARY						
M	T	W	T	F	S	S
						1
2	3	4	5	6	7	8
9	10	11	12	13	14	15
16	17	18	19	20	21	22
23	24	25	26	27	28	

JANUARY

12 MONDAY ○

Roast beef, yorkshire pudding
Roast potatoes, roast parsnips, brussel sprouts

Lamb cutlets, red currant jelly.
creamed potatoes carrots & peas.

13 TUESDAY

Pork chops, apple sauce, creamed
potatoes. cabbage & carrots.

Roast chicken, bread sauce, creamed potatoes
carrots & peas.
Chicken marengo, creamed potatoes, kidney beans

14 WEDNESDAY

Bacon, boiled beetroot, new potatoes, ~~peas~~
broad beans.
Tinned red salmon & salad, packet of crisps
& bread & butter.

Creme Fresh French Mustard.

15 THURSDAY
HOLIDAY, JAPAN

Beatrix Potter

08456 05 11 22 T/V

XPD

James Sharples Painter
Iron Foundry

23 FRIDAY

George Pallant

Roy Elvidge
Duke of Portland
Duke of Norfolk
Duke of Newcastle
Duke of Kingston

Black as night
Hot as Well
Sweet as Love

24 SATURDAY

Lomonosov USSR

~~Aldinita~~ Aldaniti
Bob Champion

Council Refuse Collection Centre
9152000

25 SUNDAY

The greatest oak was once a little nut
who held its ground

Lucid Dreams

Liverpool Cathedral Gilbert Scott

DECEMBER 1997						
M	T	W	T	F	S	S
1	2	3	4	5	6	7
8	9	10	11	12	13	14
15	16	17	18	19	20	21
22	23	24	25	26	27	28
29	30	31				

JANUARY 1998						
M	T	W	T	F	S	S
			1	2	3	4
5	6	7	8	9	10	11
12	13	14	15	16	17	18
19	20	21	22	23	24	25
26	27	28	29	30	31	

FEBRUARY						
M	T	W	T	F	S	S
						1
2	3	4	5	6	7	8
9	10	11	12	13	14	15
16	17	18	19	20	21	22
23	24	25	26	27	28	

Verbascum
White Cosmos.

Greendale Oak (Cuckney?)

Garden Centre in Welbeck Abbey gardens

This brings the best of wishes
Now your special day is here
For Health,
good luck & happiness
Throughout the coming year.

NOTES

FOR COUGHS
4 oz syrup of marshmallows
8 oz sherry.

To check up on builders
ensure they are reputable by checking
they have a government quality mark
register which you can check check
by calling 0845 300 8040

A very happy
birthday, best of luck
and good health too,
Through all the days to follow
In the year ahead of you!

JANUARY

26 MONDAY
HOLIDAY, AUSTRALIA

Books are the windows through which the soul looks out.

It must be difficult to let go of something so beautiful.

27 TUESDAY

Joan Wooley

Marcus Setchell

28 WEDNESDAY ●
THREE DAY HOLIDAY BEGINS, CHINA

Saunders Waterford. 140lb Stretched
300lb.
Burnt Sienna & Cobalt Blue.

29 THURSDAY

30 FRIDAY

Wealth & power are much more likely to be the result of breeding than they are of reading

Fran Lebowitz

31 SATURDAY

Laughter is the sun that drives Winter from the human face

Victor Hugo

1 SUNDAY

Nature does not hurry, yet everything is accomplished.

He that plants trees loves others beside himself.

Thomas Fuller
(1654 - 17-34)

JANUARY							FEBRUARY							MARCH						
M	T	W	T	F	S	S	M	T	W	T	F	S	S	M	T	W	T	F	S	S
		1	2	3	4								1	30	31					1
5	6	7	8	9	10	11	2	3	4	5	6	7	8	2	3	4	5	6	7	8
12	13	14	15	16	17	18	9	10	11	12	13	14	15	9	10	11	12	13	14	15
19	20	21	22	23	24	25	16	17	18	19	20	21	22	16	17	18	19	20	21	22
26	27	28	29	30	31		23	24	25	26	27	28		23	24	25	26	27	28	29

2 MONDAY   *Lamorna Birch   Phone for badge*

If you want a dress making   CHRISANNE   WEBSITE

WWW. CHRISANNE . COM

3 TUESDAY ◑   NERELLO   PRODUCE OF ITALY
4 . 49   MASCALESE
                                 GROWER
                 SICILIA   EGIDIO FINAZZER

Bekonscot miniature village

4 WEDNESDAY

Smart water   0115 915 1940

5 THURSDAY

FEBRUARY

6 FRIDAY
HOLIDAY, NEW ZEALAND

Its easy to be humble when you're a success
The trick is to be arrogant when you're a flop.

7 SATURDAY

A birthday thats just wonderful
A fine year on the way
And everything your heart desires —
Thats what you're wished today

8 SUNDAY

Though on the sign it is written
Forbidden to pluck these blossoms -
The wind cannot read.

CATANANCHE CAERULEA
Mt. Agel above Mentone, 18th November 1899

FEBRUARY

9 MONDAY 0800 121 8000 Database —
Brough Superior

Margaret   Thine be the Glory

10 TUESDAY
Helen   Make me a' channel of Thy Peace
Christine   "   "

Aldiniti to win the Grand National
11 WEDNESDAY ○
HOLIDAY, CHINA AND JAPAN   Bob Champion

Its 4 o'clock & time for tea
& piggy's hungry as can be
12 THURSDAY He orders tarts & ginger pop
& cakes with icing on the top
A dozen buns he gobbles down
& twenty scones baked brown as brown

FEBRUARY

Audrey Oakley ❦ ❦ Paul & Janice

13 FRIDAY

Doreen Radford & Bob.
~~Margaret Boobyer~~
~~Mary Oakland~~ ✓
~~Sheila Pike~~
Doreen McCarthy
~~Pam Thompson~~ ✓

~~Cynthia~~
~~Helen~~
~~Elaine~~
~~Margery & Bill~~

14 SATURDAY

~~Margaret Cottington~~
~~Iris Robinson~~ ✓
Betty Marshall ✓
~~Jean Richards Lambert~~
Sylvia Garnett? ✓
~~Sergt Bertulis~~

~~Audrey~~
Joan
Mary
Maurice
Chris
Terry.
~~Helen~~

15 SUNDAY

~~Enid Mather~~

~~Jean~~
Guy
Gardner

Grenville Chamberlin ❦ ❦

	JANUARY								FEBRUARY								MARCH					
M	T	W	T	F	S	S		M	T	W	T	F	S	S		M	T	W	T	F	S	S
		1	2	3	4									1		30	31					1
5	6	7	8	9	10	11		2	3	4	5	6	7	8		2	3	4	5	6	7	8
12	13	14	15	16	17	18		9	10	11	12	13	14	15		9	10	11	12	13	14	15
19	20	21	22	23	24	25		16	17	18	19	20	21	22		16	17	18	19	20	21	22
26	27	28	29	30	31			23	24	25	26	27	28			23	24	25	26	27	28	29

16 MONDAY   TRACY   9 285 778   WEEK 8
HOLIDAY. USA

1-4 MON   9-12 TUES TO FRIDAY

4ᵗʰ SEPT ?

17 TUESDAY

Joe Parsons
Ashmoor
Weatherfield   MilnThorpe 04482 2619
Nackenthwaite
MilnThorpe   Waterworn Westmoreland

18 WEDNESDAY   Stone
Cumbria
LA7 7DL

19 THURSDAY ◑

With leaves of red
this flame-like plant
is such a lovely sight
The beautiful poinsettia
Fire Flower of
Holy Night

FEBRUARY

20 FRIDAY CALIFORNIA ALLSPICE
CALYCANTHUS OCCIDENTALIS.

" FLORIDUS

CAROLINA ALLSPICE

21 SATURDAY
Art Deco
Art Nouveau.

22 SUNDAY
In Hebrew David means
Beloved of God.

Lonicera implexa
Mentone, 6th May 1896

FEBRUARY

23 MONDAY

MON
TUES
WED
THURS
FRI-

Victorian LEGHE SUTHERS

£2,600

1692 Massacre of Glencoe

24 TUESDAY
SHROVE TUESDAY

Kodak Brownie V Hawk Eye.

Edith Summerskill

Garg Avis Ballet Dancer

25 WEDNESDAY
ASH WEDNESDAY

Peter Finch Oscar Wilde
Albert Finney Saturday Night & Sunday Morning
Laurence Harvey Room at The Top
David Niven Around The World in 80 days

26 THURSDAY ●

Vic Damone   Josh Ackland:

27 FRIDAY

Pansies, Lilies, Kingcups, Daisies,
Let them live upon their praises;
Long as there's a sun that sets,
Primroses will have their glory;

28 SATURDAY   Long as there are violets,
They will have a place in glory;
There's a flower that shall be mine,
'Tis the little Celandine.

1 SUNDAY
ST. DAVID'S DAY

The Church's one foundation
Aurelia

FEBRUARY						
M	T	W	T	F	S	S
						1
2	3	4	5	6	7	8
9	10	11	12	13	14	15
16	17	18	19	20	21	22
23	24	25	26	27	28	

MARCH						
M	T	W	T	F	S	S
30	31					1
2	3	4	5	6	7	8
9	10	11	12	13	14	15
16	17	18	19	20	21	22
23	24	25	26	27	28	29

APRIL						
M	T	W	T	F	S	S
		1	2	3	4	5
6	7	8	9	10	11	12
13	14	15	16	17	18	19
20	21	22	23	24	25	26
27	28	29	30			

One Look from ~~Sunset Blvd~~ **N O T E S** ❧

Bert Wallam   Julian Fellowes

Guide me O Thou Great Redeemer
Dear Lord & Father of Mankind   Repton

If I should go before the rest of you,
Break not a flower nor inscribe a stone
Nor when I am gone speak in a Sunday voice;
But be the usual selves that I have known.
Weep if you must, parting is hell,
But life goes on, so sing as well.
          Joyce Grenfell

Chancellor's:
FLAT A12 ~~#~~ b Kingston University
          " Mill
          Kingston upon Thames
          ~~KRR~~ KR2 7LB

~ NOTES ~

James & Doral Lambert
45 The Broadway
Molt Mowbray
Leics
LE 16 7 NA

Eve Peshley
103 Wootton Road
Kempston ~~Rural~~ Rural
Bedford
MK 43 9 BJ

Sylvia Benson
32 ~~Kirkby~~ Kirkham Drive
Toton
Notts
NG 9 4HG

Edward Burne Jones.   It gives me great pleasure
   R Lia..son.   to hand you my very best
                               wishes for your Birthday

              Send my very best wishes for your
I am delighted to wish you a very Happy Birthday

Affectionately yours
            Colin

2 MONDAY

Edward King of the English called
the Confessor
He reigned for 25 yrs. + devoting most
of his time to religious matters

3 TUESDAY

He built the first ~~Abbey~~ Abbey
at West-minster
He was also known as a
Great cutter of grass. & his day
is Oct-13

4 WEDNESDAY

CHOPIN NOCTURNE IN E FLAT

Minimum effort
Maximum Satisfaction

Gordon Malkin
149. Bancroft Rd

5 THURSDAY ◑

Spondon
Derby

Growing Old is Compulsory
Growing Up is Optional

MARCH

Gerard O'Donohue.

6 FRIDAY

Everything has its beauty
but not everyone sees it

A ~~man~~ husband who is busy as a bee may come back to
find his honey missing

7 SATURDAY

Miss Lucy Hayward.
Flat CA 12
Kingston University
Kingston Hill
Kingston on Thames.

8 SUNDAY
HOLIDAY, CHINA

KT2 7LB.

The quick brown fox jumped over the lazy dog.

Brough Superior ... Van Vignette.

FEBRUARY								MARCH								APRIL						
M	T	W	T	F	S	S		M	T	W	T	F	S	S		M	T	W	T	F	S	S
						1		30	31					1				1	2	3	4	5
2	3	4	5	6	7	8		2	3	4	5	6	7	8		6	7	8	9	10	11	12
9	10	11	12	13	14	15		9	10	11	12	13	14	15		13	14	15	16	17	18	19
16	17	18	19	20	21	22		16	17	18	19	20	21	22		20	21	22	23	24	25	26
23	24	25	26	27	28			23	24	25	26	27	28	29		27	28	29	30			

9 MONDAY
COMMONWEALTH DAY

Lawrence Harvey Room at the Top &
The Alamo
David Niven Around the World in 80 days
Peter Finch Tales of Oscar Wilde

10 TUESDAY Richard Gere Pretty Woman
Albert Finney Saturday night & Sunday morning
Clint Eastwood Dirty Harry
Alan Ladd Shane.

11 WEDNESDAY Stewart Granger Scaramouche. Moonfleet.
Peter O'Toole Lawrence of Arabia

12 THURSDAY
Rebecca Evans Soprano

13 FRIDAY ○

Mrs Greta Barnaby
10. Kneeton Vale
Sherwood

Susan
Lambert Hall
The Lawns Harland Way
Cottingham
N. Humberside
HU16 5SQ

14 SATURDAY

eï
Azerbaijan

All By Myself –

Benedictus   & Karl Davies

15 SUNDAY

Hamilton Brown   Vicar
Stuart Pattison   Solicitor
Nigel Colley   Dr.

Very sensible thinking
A woman of your age

Benylin Chesty Cough Original L
£4.19.

AJUGA REPTANS
Gathered in the Turin Valley, Mentone, 15th April 1885

Dial a Ride

16 MONDAY

Egg Custard Wed   Franzipan Thurs-

Geoff Bob Ted Bill Cynthia Female

Winga & Bracket

17 TUESDAY
HOLIDAY, NORTHERN IRELAND

Twin Peaks   Take my breath away

For all we know - Rosemary Clooney.

18 WEDNESDAY

I was told that you were going to put
your Mother's bungalow for sale.
If this information is correct I would be very
grateful if you could give me some idea of your
asking price. A relative of mine is very interested.
Of course I will keep this information to myself

19 THURSDAY

Benedictus by the ~~C~~ Karl Jenkins from
the Armed Man

Edward Burne Jones   *Holman Hunt*

MARCH

20 FRIDAY
VERNAL EQUINOX. SPRING BEGINS
HOLIDAY, JAPAN

Wooler Glanton Warkworth Alnmouth Morpeth

21 SATURDAY ◑

Christine & John Williams

Mrs B firm support
T 60/6032/4514

Red Green
Yellow Purple
Blue Orange .

22 SUNDAY
MOTHERING SUNDAY

Do not wake a sleeping tiger

FEBRUARY								MARCH								APRIL						
M	T	W	T	F	S	S		M	T	W	T	F	S	S		M	T	W	T	F	S	S
						1		30	31					1				1	2	3	4	5
2	3	4	5	6	7	8		2	3	4	5	6	7	8		6	7	8	9	10	11	12
9	10	11	12	13	14	15		9	10	11	12	13	14	15		13	14	15	16	17	18	19
16	17	18	19	20	21	22		16	17	18	19	20	21	22		20	21	22	23	24	25	26
23	24	25	26	27	28			23	24	25	26	27	28	29		27	28	29	30			

23 MONDAY

Around the World in 80 days   David Niven

Room at the Top   Lawrence Harvey

Saturday Night Sunday Morning   Sally Ann Field

24 TUESDAY

Affect means to cause a change

Effect means a result.

25 WEDNESDAY

To live in hearts we leave
behind is not to die

26 THURSDAY

It is the intrinsic lack of appreciation
of open space & its importance to
our environment at local level
that we must fight

27 FRIDAY

*Heaven hath no rage
like love to hatred turned
nor Hell a fury
like a woman scorned*
   William... Congreve

28 SATURDAY ●

*Back of the shack
where the black eyed
Susan's grow*

29 SUNDAY
BRITISH SUMMER TIME BEGINS. UK

*Simplicity is the
essence of style*

*Isaac Walton
John Ball
Jensen*

Thermal.

PRIMULA X VARIABILIS
From the North Side of Gran Monti, Mentone, 12th April 1899

30 MONDAY

I would like to know why residents living in the vicinity of the Bramcote Lane Shops are only just aware that an application to demolish two bungalows & build on a new store & car park on Bramcote Lane

31 TUESDAY

was made to the Council on June 30th. I have lived here for 31 years. In that time we have had anti-social behaviour, problems with but with the help of Georgina Culley that has been iradicated however I can see it happening again if a new

1 WEDNESDAY

large store is allowed to keep very late hours.

We are very proud of our parade of shops on Bramcote Lane & they all give excellent service. Surely we should give consideration

2 THURSDAY

to the residents living on Bramcote Lane

Yours faithfully.

APRIL

3 FRIDAY ◐

Art Group

Geoff Breedon
Frank
Bob Johnson
Cynthia

Brief Encounter

Longleat
Marquess of Bath

4 SATURDAY

M.O.G's
Doreen Parry
Val
Enid Mather
Enid's Friend

5 SUNDAY

PALM SUNDAY
HOLIDAY. CHINA
DST BEGINS. USA

Jean Bond
Ann Broadbent   Manley Ave

NOTES

Chicken Kiev
Flatten chicken breast
Filling Butter
Grated cheese
Parsley Spring Onions
Roll chicken in flour, egg
breadcrumbs & fry for 15 mins

Coleridge
He prayeth best who love'th best
all creature great & small

Friendship is like wetting your pants
Everyone can see it
but only you can feel it's warmth

NOTES

Friday 24ᵗʰ Sept.
Mon. Aug 30ᵗʰ

Greatwood.   GREATWOOD

Chancers Canterbury Tales
Cut out picture on Staircase

Alan Ladd Shane
Tyrone Power The Mask of Zorro
William Holden Sunset Blvd, Sabrina

Life I believe is not a dream
So dark as sages say;
Oft a little morning rain
Foretells a pleasant day;
Sometimes there are clouds of gloom,
But these a Transient all;
If the rain makes the roses g bloom
Oh why lament its fall?

APRIL

6 MONDAY

7 TUESDAY

8 WEDNESDAY

9 THURSDAY

APRIL

XXIII

10 FRIDAY
GOOD FRIDAY HOLIDAY. UK. AUSTRALIA. CANADA. NEW ZEALAND AND GERMANY

*Oh, make the most of what we
yet may spend,
Before we too into the Dust
descend,*

11 SATURDAY ○
FIRST DAY OF PASSOVER (PESACH)
HOLIDAY. AUSTRALIA

*Dust into Dust and under
Dust to lie,
Sans Wine, sans Song, sans
Singer, and — sans End!*

12 SUNDAY
EASTER SUNDAY

MARCH						
M	T	W	T	F	S	S
30	31					1
2	3	4	5	6	7	8
9	10	11	12	13	14	15
16	17	18	19	20	21	22
23	24	25	26	27	28	29

APRIL						
M	T	W	T	F	S	S
		1	2	3	4	5
6	7	8	9	10	11	12
13	14	15	16	17	18	19
20	21	22	23	24	25	26
27	28	29	30			

MAY						
M	T	W	T	F	S	S
				1	2	3
4	5	6	7	8	9	10
11	12	13	14	15	16	17
18	19	20	21	22	23	24
25	26	27	28	29	30	31

APRIL

13 MONDAY

HOLIDAY, UK EXC SCOTLAND, FRANCE, ITALY, GERMANY, AUSTRALIA, NEW ZEALAND AND CANADA

WEEK 16

14 TUESDAY

15 WEDNESDAY

16 THURSDAY

APRIL

17 FRIDAY

18 SATURDAY

19 SUNDAY ◑

MUSCARI NEGLECTUM
Gathered at Mentone, 10th March 1876

APRIL

20 MONDAY

---

21 TUESDAY
BIRTHDAY OF QUEEN ELIZABETH II

---

22 WEDNESDAY

---

23 THURSDAY
ST. GEORGE'S DAY

APRIL

24 FRIDAY

HOLIDAY, ITALY

25 SATURDAY

26 SUNDAY ●

<table>
<tr><td colspan="7">MARCH</td><td colspan="7">APRIL</td><td colspan="7">MAY</td></tr>
<tr><td>M</td><td>T</td><td>W</td><td>T</td><td>F</td><td>S</td><td>S</td><td>M</td><td>T</td><td>W</td><td>T</td><td>F</td><td>S</td><td>S</td><td>M</td><td>T</td><td>W</td><td>T</td><td>F</td><td>S</td><td>S</td></tr>
<tr><td>30</td><td>31</td><td></td><td></td><td></td><td></td><td>1</td><td></td><td></td><td>1</td><td>2</td><td>3</td><td>4</td><td>5</td><td></td><td></td><td></td><td></td><td>1</td><td>2</td><td>3</td></tr>
<tr><td>2</td><td>3</td><td>4</td><td>5</td><td>6</td><td>7</td><td>8</td><td>6</td><td>7</td><td>8</td><td>9</td><td>10</td><td>11</td><td>12</td><td>4</td><td>5</td><td>6</td><td>7</td><td>8</td><td>9</td><td>10</td></tr>
<tr><td>9</td><td>10</td><td>11</td><td>12</td><td>13</td><td>14</td><td>15</td><td>13</td><td>14</td><td>15</td><td>16</td><td>17</td><td>18</td><td>19</td><td>11</td><td>12</td><td>13</td><td>14</td><td>15</td><td>16</td><td>17</td></tr>
<tr><td>16</td><td>17</td><td>18</td><td>19</td><td>20</td><td>21</td><td>22</td><td>20</td><td>21</td><td>22</td><td>23</td><td>24</td><td>25</td><td>26</td><td>18</td><td>19</td><td>20</td><td>21</td><td>22</td><td>23</td><td>24</td></tr>
<tr><td>23</td><td>24</td><td>25</td><td>26</td><td>27</td><td>28</td><td>29</td><td>27</td><td>28</td><td>29</td><td>30</td><td></td><td></td><td></td><td>25</td><td>26</td><td>27</td><td>28</td><td>29</td><td>30</td><td>31</td></tr>
</table>

NOTES

NOTES

APRIL

27 MONDAY

WEEK 18

HOLIDAY, AUSTRALIA

28 TUESDAY

ISLAMIC NEW YEAR BEGINS

29 WEDNESDAY

HOLIDAY, JAPAN

30 THURSDAY

MAY

---

1 FRIDAY

HOLIDAY, FRANCE, GERMANY, ITALY AND CHINA

---

2 SATURDAY

---

3 SUNDAY ◗

HOLIDAY, JAPAN

	APRIL					
M	T	W	T	F	S	S
	1	2	3	4	5
6	7	8	9	10	11	12
13	14	15	16	17	18	19
20	21	22	23	24	25	26
27	28	29	30

	MAY					
M	T	W	T	F	S	S
				1	2	3
4	5	6	7	8	9	10
11	12	13	14	15	16	17
18	19	20	21	22	23	24
25	26	27	28	29	30	31

	JUNE					
M	T	W	T	F	S	S
1	2	3	4	5	6	7
8	9	10	11	12	13	14
15	16	17	18	19	20	21
22	23	24	25	26	27	28
29	30

∾ MAY ∾

4 MONDAY   WEEK 19
HOLIDAY, UK (TBC)

5 TUESDAY
HOLIDAY, JAPAN

6 WEDNESDAY

7 THURSDAY

MAY

8 FRIDAY

HOLIDAY, FRANCE

9 SATURDAY

10 SUNDAY

Narcissus tazetta
From San Remo, 27th February 1888

MAY

11 MONDAY ○   WEEK 20

12 TUESDAY

13 WEDNESDAY

14 THURSDAY

15 FRIDAY

16 SATURDAY

17 SUNDAY

	APRIL								MAY								JUNE					
M	T	W	T	F	S	S	M	T	W	T	F	S	S	M	T	W	T	F	S	S
	1	2	3	4	5					1	2	3	1	2	3	4	5	6	7
6	7	8	9	10	11	12	4	5	6	7	8	9	10	8	9	10	11	12	13	14
13	14	15	16	17	18	19	11	12	13	14	15	16	17	15	16	17	18	19	20	21
20	21	22	23	24	25	26	18	19	20	21	22	23	24	22	23	24	25	26	27	28
27	28	29	30				25	26	27	28	29	30	31	29	30					

MAY

18 MONDAY

WEEK 21

HOLIDAY, CANADA

19 TUESDAY ◑

20 WEDNESDAY

21 THURSDAY

HOLIDAY, FRANCE AND GERMANY

22 FRIDAY

23 SATURDAY

24 SUNDAY

CENTRANTHUS RUBER
Gorbio Valley, Mentone, 24th April 1896

M A Y

25 MONDAY ●

HOLIDAY. UK AND USA

26 TUESDAY

27 WEDNESDAY

28 THURSDAY

MAY

❧ ∼ **M A Y** ∼ ❧

◆

29 FRIDAY

◆

30 SATURDAY
HOLIDAY, CHINA

◆

31 SUNDAY,
FEAST OF WEEKS (SHAVUOT), WHIT SUNDAY

◆

APRIL						
M	T	W	T	F	S	S
	1	2	3	4	5	
6	7	8	9	10	11	12
13	14	15	16	17	18	19
20	21	22	23	24	25	26
27	28	29	30			

MAY						
M	T	W	T	F	S	S
				1	2	3
4	5	6	7	8	9	10
11	12	13	14	15	16	17
18	19	20	21	22	23	24
25	26	27	28	29	30	31

JUNE						
M	T	W	T	F	S	S
1	2	3	4	5	6	7
8	9	10	11	12	13	14
15	16	17	18	19	20	21
22	23	24	25	26	27	28
29	30					

◆

NOTES

NOTES

J U N E

1 MONDAY

WEEK 23

HOLIDAY, NEW ZEALAND, FRANCE AND GERMANY

2 TUESDAY ◑

3 WEDNESDAY

4 THURSDAY

JUNE

5 FRIDAY
HOLIDAY, CHINA

6 SATURDAY

7 SUNDAY

			MAY								JUNE								JULY			
M	T	W	T	F	S	S	M	T	W	T	F	S	S	M	T	W	T	F	S	S
				1	2	3														
				1	2	3	1	2	3	4	5	6	7		1	2	3	4	5
4	5	6	7	8	9	10	8	9	10	11	12	13	14	6	7	8	9	10	11	12
11	12	13	14	15	16	17	15	16	17	18	19	20	21	13	14	15	16	17	18	19
18	19	20	21	22	23	24	22	23	24	25	26	27	28	20	21	22	23	24	25	26
25	26	27	28	29	30	31	29	30						27	28	29	30	31		

J U N E

8 MONDAY

9 TUESDAY

10 WEDNESDAY ○

BIRTHDAY OF PRINCE PHILIP, DUKE OF EDINBURGH

11 THURSDAY

J U N E

12 FRIDAY

13 SATURDAY
THE QUEEN'S OFFICIAL BIRTHDAY (TBC)

14 SUNDAY

Vinca difformis (V. acutiflora)
From the road to Rocca Bruna near Mentone, 25th February 1878

J U N E

15 MONDAY

HOLIDAY, AUSTRALIA

16 TUESDAY

17 WEDNESDAY ☽

18 THURSDAY

JUNE

19 FRIDAY

20 SATURDAY

21 SUNDAY

SUMMER SOLSTICE, SUMMER BEGINS
FATHER'S DAY, UK

MAY						
M	T	W	T	F	S	S
				1	2	3
4	5	6	7	8	9	10
11	12	13	14	15	16	17
18	19	20	21	22	23	24
25	26	27	28	29	30	31

JUNE						
M	T	W	T	F	S	S
1	2	3	4	5	6	7
8	9	10	11	12	13	14
15	16	17	18	19	20	21
22	23	24	25	26	27	28
29	30					

JULY						
M	T	W	T	F	S	S
		1	2	3	4	5
6	7	8	9	10	11	12
13	14	15	16	17	18	19
20	21	22	23	24	25	26
27	28	29	30	31		

J U N E

22 MONDAY

23 TUESDAY

24 WEDNESDAY ●

25 THURSDAY

26 FRIDAY

27 SATURDAY

28 SUNDAY

ROSA CANINA
Gathered in the Gorbio Valley, Mentone, 10th May 1897

JUNE-JULY

29 MONDAY

30 TUESDAY

1 WEDNESDAY ◖
HOLIDAY, CANADA

2 THURSDAY

JULY

3 FRIDAY

4 SATURDAY

5 SUNDAY

			JUNE			
M	T	W	T	F	S	S
1	2	3	4	5	6	7
8	9	10	11	12	13	14
15	16	17	18	19	20	21
22	23	24	25	26	27	28
29	30					

			JULY			
M	T	W	T	F	S	S
		1	2	3	4	5
6	7	8	9	10	11	12
13	14	15	16	17	18	19
20	21	22	23	24	25	26
27	28	29	30	31		

			AUGUST			
M	T	W	T	F	S	S
31					1	2
3	4	5	6	7	8	9
10	11	12	13	14	15	16
17	18	19	20	21	22	23
24	25	26	27	28	29	30

NOTES

NOTES

JULY

6 MONDAY

7 TUESDAY

8 WEDNESDAY

9 THURSDAY ○

JULY

10 FRIDAY

11 SATURDAY

12 SUNDAY

JUNE						
M	T	W	T	F	S	S
1	2	3	4	5	6	7
8	9	10	11	12	13	14
15	16	17	18	19	20	21
22	23	24	25	26	27	28
29	30					

JULY						
M	T	W	T	F	S	S
		1	2	3	4	5
6	7	8	9	10	11	12
13	14	15	16	17	18	19
20	21	22	23	24	25	26
27	28	29	30	31		

AUGUST						
M	T	W	T	F	S	S
31					1	2
3	4	5	6	7	8	9
10	11	12	13	14	15	16
17	18	19	20	21	22	23
24	25	26	27	28	29	30

JULY

13 MONDAY

HOLIDAY, NORTHERN IRELAND (TBC)

14 TUESDAY

HOLIDAY, FRANCE

15 WEDNESDAY

16 THURSDAY ◑

17 FRIDAY

18 SATURDAY

19 SUNDAY

SERAPIAS CORDIGERA
Gathered near Albenga, 15th April 1881

J U L Y

20 MONDAY
HOLIDAY, JAPAN

WEEK 30

21 TUESDAY

22 WEDNESDAY

23 THURSDAY ●

24 FRIDAY

25 SATURDAY

26 SUNDAY

	JUNE								JULY								AUGUST					
M	T	W	T	F	S	S		M	T	W	T	F	S	S		M	T	W	T	F	S	S
1	2	3	4	5	6	7			1	2	3	4	5		31					1	2
8	9	10	11	12	13	14		6	7	8	9	10	11	12		3	4	5	6	7	8	9
15	16	17	18	19	20	21		13	14	15	16	17	18	19		10	11	12	13	14	15	16
22	23	24	25	26	27	28		20	21	22	23	24	25	26		17	18	19	20	21	22	23
29	30							27	28	29	30	31				24	25	26	27	28	29	30

NOTES

NOTES

JULY

27 MONDAY

28 TUESDAY

29 WEDNESDAY

30 THURSDAY

31 FRIDAY ◐

1 SATURDAY

2 SUNDAY

JULY						
M	T	W	T	F	S	S
	1	2	3	4	5	
6	7	8	9	10	11	12
13	14	15	16	17	18	19
20	21	22	23	24	25	26
27	28	29	30	31		

AUGUST						
M	T	W	T	F	S	S
31					1	2
3	4	5	6	7	8	9
10	11	12	13	14	15	16
17	18	19	20	21	22	23
24	25	26	27	28	29	30

SEPTEMBER						
M	T	W	T	F	S	S
1	2	3	4	5	6	
7	8	9	10	11	12	13
14	15	16	17	18	19	20
21	22	23	24	25	26	27
28	29	30				

AUGUST

3 MONDAY

HOLIDAY, SCOTLAND

4 TUESDAY

5 WEDNESDAY

6 THURSDAY

7 FRIDAY

8 SATURDAY ○

9 SUNDAY

CAMPANULA MACRORHIZA
Gathered near the Pont St Louis, Mentone, 5th December 1881

AUGUST

10 MONDAY

11 TUESDAY

12 WEDNESDAY

13 THURSDAY

AUGUST

14 FRIDAY ◑

15 SATURDAY
HOLIDAY, ITALY

16 SUNDAY

			JULY							AUGUST								SEPTEMBER				
M	T	W	T	F	S	S	M	T	W	T	F	S	S	M	T	W	T	F	S	S
	1	2	3	4	5	31				1	2		1	2	3	4	5	6
6	7	8	9	10	11	12	3	4	5	6	7	8	9	7	8	9	10	11	12	13
13	14	15	16	17	18	19	10	11	12	13	14	15	16	14	15	16	17	18	19	20
20	21	22	23	24	25	26	17	18	19	20	21	22	23	21	22	23	24	25	26	27
27	28	29	30	31			24	25	26	27	28	29	30	28	29	30

AUGUST

17 MONDAY

18 TUESDAY

19 WEDNESDAY

20 THURSDAY

AUGUST

21 FRIDAY

22 SATURDAY ●

23 SUNDAY

ANEMONE PAVONINA
Gathered in the Gorbio Valley, Mentone, 15th March 1881

AUGUST

24 MONDAY

25 TUESDAY

26 WEDNESDAY

27 THURSDAY

AUGUST

28 FRIDAY

29 SATURDAY

30 SUNDAY ☽

		JULY				
M	T	W	T	F	S	S
	1	2	3	4	5	
6	7	8	9	10	11	12
13	14	15	16	17	18	19
20	21	22	23	24	25	26
27	28	29	30	31		

		AUGUST				
M	T	W	T	F	S	S
31					1	2
3	4	5	6	7	8	9
10	11	12	13	14	15	16
17	18	19	20	21	22	23
24	25	26	27	28	29	30

		SEPTEMBER				
M	T	W	T	F	S	S
1	2	3	4	5	6	
7	8	9	10	11	12	13
14	15	16	17	18	19	20
21	22	23	24	25	26	27
28	29	30				

NOTES

NOTES

31 MONDAY
HOLIDAY, UK EXC SCOTLAND

1 TUESDAY

2 WEDNESDAY

3 THURSDAY

SEPTEMBER

4 FRIDAY

5 SATURDAY
HOLIDAY, CHINA

6 SUNDAY ○

AUGUST						
M	T	W	T	F	S	S
31					1	2
3	4	5	6	7	8	9
10	11	12	13	14	15	16
17	18	19	20	21	22	23
24	25	26	27	28	29	30

SEPTEMBER						
M	T	W	T	F	S	S
	1	2	3	4	5	6
7	8	9	10	11	12	13
14	15	16	17	18	19	20
21	22	23	24	25	26	27
28	29	30				

OCTOBER						
M	T	W	T	F	S	S
			1	2	3	4
5	6	7	8	9	10	11
12	13	14	15	16	17	18
19	20	21	22	23	24	25
26	27	28	29	30	31	

SEPTEMBER

7 MONDAY

HOLIDAY, USA AND CANADA

8 TUESDAY

9 WEDNESDAY

10 THURSDAY

SEPTEMBER

11 FRIDAY

12 SATURDAY

13 SUNDAY ◑

VIOLA ARENARIA
Mentone, 22nd March 1893

SEPTEMBER

14 MONDAY

15 TUESDAY

HOLIDAY, JAPAN

16 WEDNESDAY

17 THURSDAY

SEPTEMBER

18 FRIDAY

19 SATURDAY

20 SUNDAY ●

AUGUST						
M	T	W	T	F	S	S
31				1	2
3	4	5	6	7	8	9
10	11	12	13	14	15	16
17	18	19	20	21	22	23
24	25	26	27	28	29	30

SEPTEMBER						
M	T	W	T	F	S	S
	1	2	3	4	5	6
7	8	9	10	11	12	13
14	15	16	17	18	19	20
21	22	23	24	25	26	27
28	29	30				

OCTOBER						
M	T	W	T	F	S	S
			1	2	3	4
5	6	7	8	9	10	11
12	13	14	15	16	17	18
19	20	21	22	23	24	25
26	27	28	29	30	31	

S E P T E M B E R

21 MONDAY

JEWISH NEW YEAR (ROSH HASHANAH)

22 TUESDAY

23 WEDNESDAY

AUTUMNAL EQUINOX, AUTUMN BEGINS
HOLIDAY, JAPAN

24 THURSDAY

25 FRIDAY

26 SATURDAY

27 SUNDAY

ASTER SEDIFOLIUS (A. ACRIS)
Gathered at Mentone, 23rd November 1878

28 MONDAY ◑

29 TUESDAY

30 WEDNESDAY

DAY OF ATONEMENT (YOM KIPPUR)

1 THURSDAY

HOLIDAY, CHINA

OCTOBER

2 FRIDAY

3 SATURDAY
HOLIDAY, GERMANY

4 SUNDAY

SEPTEMBER						
M	T	W	T	F	S	S
	1	2	3	4	5	6
7	8	9	10	11	12	13
14	15	16	17	18	19	20
21	22	23	24	25	26	27
28	29	30				

OCTOBER						
M	T	W	T	F	S	S
			1	2	3	4
5	6	7	8	9	10	11
12	13	14	15	16	17	18
19	20	21	22	23	24	25
26	27	28	29	30	31	

NOVEMBER						
M	T	W	T	F	S	S
30						1
2	3	4	5	6	7	8
9	10	11	12	13	14	15
16	17	18	19	20	21	22
23	24	25	26	27	28	29

NOTES

NOTES

OCTOBER

5 MONDAY ○
FIRST DAY OF TABERNACLES (SUCCOTH)

6 TUESDAY

7 WEDNESDAY

8 THURSDAY

OCTOBER

9 FRIDAY

10 SATURDAY
HOLIDAY, JAPAN

11 SUNDAY

SEPTEMBER								OCTOBER								NOVEMBER						
M	T	W	T	F	S	S		M	T	W	T	F	S	S		M	T	W	T	F	S	S
	1	2	3	4	5	6					1	2	3	4		30						1
7	8	9	10	11	12	13		5	6	7	8	9	10	11		2	3	4	5	6	7	8
14	15	16	17	18	19	20		12	13	14	15	16	17	18		9	10	11	12	13	14	15
21	22	23	24	25	26	27		19	20	21	22	23	24	25		16	17	18	19	20	21	22
28	29	30						26	27	28	29	30	31			23	24	25	26	27	28	29

OCTOBER

12 MONDAY ◑

WEEK 42

HOLIDAY, USA AND CANADA

13 TUESDAY

14 WEDNESDAY

15 THURSDAY

16 FRIDAY

17 SATURDAY

18 SUNDAY

CENTAUREA CYANUS
Gathered on the road to Frejus, 28th April 1882

OCTOBER

19 MONDAY

20 TUESDAY ●

21 WEDNESDAY

22 THURSDAY

OCTOBER

23 FRIDAY

24 SATURDAY

25 SUNDAY
BRITISH SUMMER TIME ENDS, UK
DST ENDS, USA

SEPTEMBER							OCTOBER							NOVEMBER						
M	T	W	T	F	S	S	M	T	W	T	F	S	S	M	T	W	T	F	S	S
	1	2	3	4	5	6				1	2	3	4	30						1
7	8	9	10	11	12	13	5	6	7	8	9	10	11	2	3	4	5	6	7	8
14	15	16	17	18	19	20	12	13	14	15	16	17	18	9	10	11	12	13	14	15
21	22	23	24	25	26	27	19	20	21	22	23	24	25	16	17	18	19	20	21	22
28	29	30					26	27	28	29	30	31		23	24	25	26	27	28	29

NOTES

NOTES

OCTOBER

26 MONDAY

HOLIDAY, NEW ZEALAND

27 TUESDAY

28 WEDNESDAY ◐

29 THURSDAY

OCTOBER – NOVEMBER

30 FRIDAY

31 SATURDAY

1 SUNDAY
ALL SAINTS DAY

OCTOBER						
M	T	W	T	F	S	S
			1	2	3	4
5	6	7	8	9	10	11
12	13	14	15	16	17	18
19	20	21	22	23	24	25
26	27	28	29	30	31	

NOVEMBER						
M	T	W	T	F	S	S
30						1
2	3	4	5	6	7	8
9	10	11	12	13	14	15
16	17	18	19	20	21	22
23	24	25	26	27	28	29

DECEMBER						
M	T	W	T	F	S	S
	1	2	3	4	5	6
7	8	9	10	11	12	13
14	15	16	17	18	19	20
21	22	23	24	25	26	27
28	29	30	31			

NOVEMBER

2 MONDAY

---

3 TUESDAY

HOLIDAY, JAPAN

---

4 WEDNESDAY ○

---

5 THURSDAY

NOVEMBER

6 FRIDAY

7 SATURDAY

8 SUNDAY

REMEMBRANCE SUNDAY

DIANTHUS, SP.
From Beaulieu Alpes Maritimes, 12th November 1894

NOVEMBER

9 MONDAY

10 TUESDAY

11 WEDNESDAY ◑
HOLIDAY, USA, CANADA AND FRANCE

12 THURSDAY

NOVEMBER

13 FRIDAY

14 SATURDAY
BIRTHDAY OF THE PRINCE OF WALES

15 SUNDAY

OCTOBER						
M	T	W	T	F	S	S
		1	2	3	4	
5	6	7	8	9	10	11
12	13	14	15	16	17	18
19	20	21	22	23	24	25
26	27	28	29	30	31	

NOVEMBER						
M	T	W	T	F	S	S
30						1
2	3	4	5	6	7	8
9	10	11	12	13	14	15
16	17	18	19	20	21	22
23	24	25	26	27	28	29

DECEMBER						
M	T	W	T	F	S	S
	1	2	3	4	5	6
7	8	9	10	11	12	13
14	15	16	17	18	19	20
21	22	23	24	25	26	27
28	29	30	31			

NOVEMBER

16 MONDAY

17 TUESDAY

18 WEDNESDAY

19 THURSDAY ●

NOVEMBER

20 FRIDAY

21 SATURDAY

22 SUNDAY

LAVATERA ARBOREA, TREE MALLOW
Mentone, 19th May 1900

NOVEMBER

23 MONDAY
HOLIDAY, JAPAN

On Friday 5ᵗʰ Aug 2011

I sold my car Honda Civic to Adam Staniforth
71, Stenson Road Derby. born 3-10-1991

1343 cc

24 TUESDAY

2 Axle Rigid Body   F634 HNL.

Chassis frame no JHMEC 84200S009948

Engine no D 13B11011395

Silver   1ˢᵗ Reg - 18-8-1988

25 WEDNESDAY

26 THURSDAY
HOLIDAY, USA

NOVEMBER

27 FRIDAY ◑

28 SATURDAY

29 SUNDAY
FIRST SUNDAY IN ADVENT

OCTOBER						
M	T	W	T	F	S	S
		1	2	3	4	
5	6	7	8	9	10	11
12	13	14	15	16	17	18
19	20	21	22	23	24	25
26	27	28	29	30	31	

NOVEMBER						
M	T	W	T	F	S	S
30						1
2	3	4	5	6	7	8
9	10	11	12	13	14	15
16	17	18	19	20	21	22
23	24	25	26	27	28	29

DECEMBER						
M	T	W	T	F	S	S
	1	2	3	4	5	6
7	8	9	10	11	12	13
14	15	16	17	18	19	20
21	22	23	24	25	26	27
28	29	30	31			

NOTES

Daphne Butkwoodii

Fuchsia

Hydrangea

Edward Coley Burne-Jones

Holman Hunt

Milais

~~Ruth & George Meachim~~

~~Margaret Reddish~~

Brenda & Steve Cooper

Dottie Miller

Ken & Angie Pain

Terry Davie · John Barber

Margaret Bellamy

Janice & Raymond

Cousin June & Dave

Joyce & ~~John~~ Morgan

NOTES

Guy Benson. Positive Solutions Ltd

K. class — Jean, Karen, Brenda,

Joan, Maurice Mary.

Christine & David.

Linda & Adam

Susan & Jack

John Wiltshee & Christine

Sheila Clifton

Margaret Boobyer

Jean & Arthur — Pat & Arthur

Freda Belshaw

Andrew & Christine McCarthy

Joan & Bernard Brooks

Margery Heafe Betty Withers

Joan Fisher Nora Groome

Sheila Pike Iris Best

Sylvia Garnett, Betty Marshall

Pam Thompson; Joan Forman

Elaine Whitby. Alma & Griff

Bob & Carolyn. Radford.

Jean Lambert David Singleton

30 MONDAY

ST. ANDREW'S DAY

State Pension

```
103 - 49          166 - 00     48 - 93
103 - 49           99 - 90      Jan 2010
103 - 49           36 - 00
103 - 49          301 - 90
413 - 96
301 - 90                    52/715/86      12 × 715 - 86
715 - 86

                           166. 41
                            40   52 50    41 50    24 - 95   24 - 99
                                 52 50    41 50    24 - 95   24 - 99
                           169       41 50    24 - 95   24 - 99
                                 41 50    24 - 95   24 - 9
```

412
1 - 96
413 96

23
92

1 TUESDAY

```
103 - 49          178 - 98     166 - 0    24 - 95    24 - 9
 41 - 50           12 - 23      48 - 93   99 30      99 9
 24 - 99          191 - 21               12 - 23
  9 - 00
178 - 98
178 - 98
```

2 WEDNESDAY

3 THURSDAY ○

11 FRIDAY

48 - 93
39

48.93
5

204.65
4

48
39
1440
432
1872
36 - 27
10
1908 - 37

2790
837
3627
244 - 65
244 - 65
489 - 30
489

489 . 30
489 - 30
489 - 30
10
440 - 37
1908 - 37
48 - 93
1957 - 30

12 SATURDAY

48 - 93

489 - 30
48 . 93
440 - 37

480
9 - 30
489 - 30

48 - 93
48 . 93
97 86

48 . 93
1957 - 30

13 SUNDAY

2006   5 months
2007
2008
2009
2010   1 payment

1761 - 48   3 yr
244 - 65   5 months
2010

489 - 30
97 - 86
587 - 16   07
587 - 16   08
587 - 16   09
1761 - 48
2

ANEMONE CORONARIA
Mentone, 4th March 1881

14 MONDAY

Friday Picnic Pork Pie — Jam Doughnut

15 TUESDAY

16 WEDNESDAY

17 THURSDAY

DECEMBER

18 FRIDAY ●

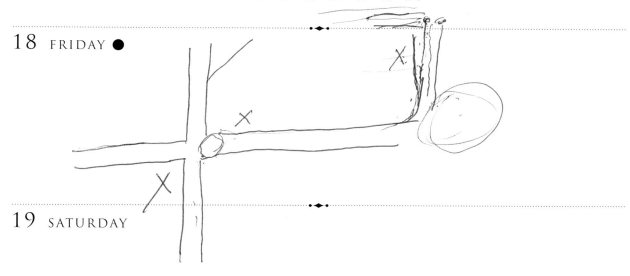

19 SATURDAY

20 SUNDAY
FIRST DAY OF RAMADAN

	NOVEMBER								DECEMBER 1998								JANUARY 1999					
M	T	W	T	F	S	S	M	T	W	T	F	S	S	M	T	W	T	F	S	S
30						1		1	2	3	4	5	6					1	2	3
2	3	4	5	6	7	8	7	8	9	10	11	12	13	4	5	6	7	8	9	10
9	10	11	12	13	14	15	14	15	16	17	18	19	20	11	12	13	14	15	16	17
16	17	18	19	20	21	22	21	22	23	24	25	26	27	18	19	20	21	22	23	24
23	24	25	26	27	28	29	28	29	30	31				25	26	27	28	29	30	31

DECEMBER

21 MONDAY 29·10·07

Early afternoon recorded message
wanting to help me with my debts.
                30·10·07

12·Noon Wanting to help me with
    my debts.

22 TUESDAY 30·10·07
WINTER SOLSTICE, WINTER BEGINS

12·40 PM Some recorded message
        1/2/08

13-17 Home Improvements no phone number.

23 WEDNESDAY LIVERPOOL.   Hope St Hotel.
HOLIDAY, JAPAN
    The London Carriage Works. (Restaurant)

    Faulkner Street (Cobbled).

24 THURSDAY
CHRISTMAS EVE

DECEMBER

25 FRIDAY 2·10·07
CHRISTMAS DAY

10AM   08447739922 · Recorded message · regarding debts ·

3·10·07
2·29PM   08004929922   SOUNDED ASIAN   PUT PHONE DOWN

---

26 SATURDAY ◑
BOXING DAY

4·10·07

12·47PM   08004969922

SAID HELLO NOBODY ANSWERED

1·57

---

27 SUNDAY   A RECORDED MESSAGE
SAY THEY ARE A MORTGAGE PROVIDER
8·10·07
14·25
08004969922

FEMALE VOICE ASKING ME TO ANSWER
THREE QUESTIONS.

12·10·07
2·20pm
08004969922.

18·10·07
11·07AM ·

DAPHNE MEZEREUM
From a wood at the base of Mt. Razel, Mentone, 20th March 1896

08702209317 DIDN'T SPEAK.

28 MONDAY
HOLIDAY. UK

I will not require the services of Green Thumb any more. In future my gardener will treat my lawns in between cutting the grass & clearing up etc.

Thank you for your past services

Yours faithfully

Audrey Oakley (Mrs)

29 TUESDAY

30 WEDNESDAY

Trans urethral resection of a bladder tumour (TURB

31 THURSDAY

JANUARY

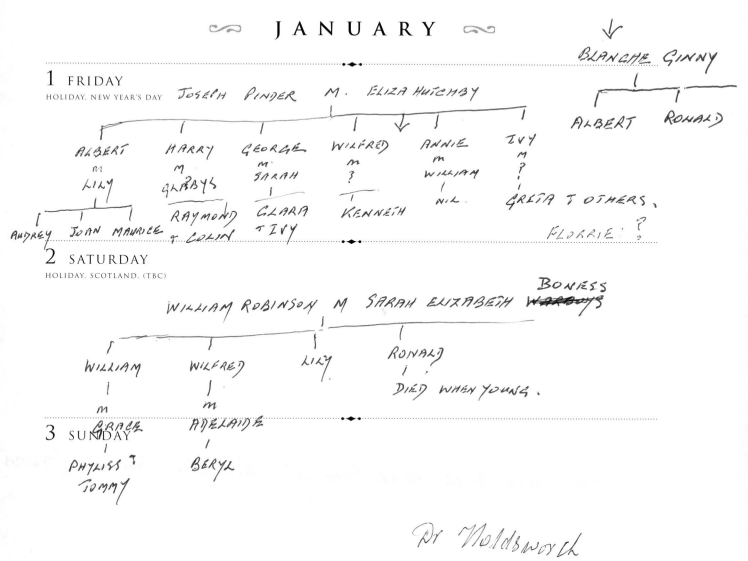

1 FRIDAY
HOLIDAY, NEW YEAR'S DAY

JOSEPH PINDER   M. ELIZA HUTCHBY

ALBERT   HARRY   GEORGE   WILFRED   ANNIE   IVY
m   m   m   m   m   m
LILY   GLADYS   SARAH   ?   WILLIAM   ?
                                                                 GRETA & OTHERS.

AUDREY JOAN MAURICE   RAYMOND   CLARA   KENNETH   N.L.   FLORRIE ?
                       & COLIN   & IVY

BLANCHE GINNY
ALBERT   RONALD

2 SATURDAY
HOLIDAY, SCOTLAND, (TBC)

WILLIAM ROBINSON M SARAH ELIZABETH ~~WARBOYS~~ BONESS

WILLIAM   WILFRED   LILY   RONALD
m   m   DIED WHEN YOUNG.
GRACE   ADELAIDE

3 SUNDAY

PHYLISS &   BERYL
TOMMY

Dr Woldsworth

MENUS.

~ FORWARD PLANNER ~

JANUARY
Hot smoked salmon
Chips

FEBRUARY
Peas & celery in white sauce.

MARCH
Casserole steak
Mashed potato or

APRIL
Yorkshire puddings

MAY
Barnsley chops
Mashed potato
Carrots

JUNE
Peas.

Soup.
JULY
Tinned Salmon
Salad
Bread & Butter

AUGUST
Cheese omelet
Grilled tomatoes
Bread & Butter

SEPTEMBER

OCTOBER
Chicken parcel
Greens.

NOVEMBER

DECEMBER

ADDRESSES

NAME *Easter cards*

ADDRESS

Margaret Boobyer

TELEPHONE *Margaret Reddish*

NAME *Alma & Griff*

ADDRESS *Jean*

Janice

TELEPHONE *Joan*

Maurice

NAME

ADDRESS *Christine*

Margery

TELEPHONE

NAME

ADDRESS

TELEPHONE

NAME

ADDRESS

TELEPHONE

NAME

ADDRESS

TELEPHONE

NAME

ADDRESS

TELEPHONE

NAME

ADDRESS

TELEPHONE

NAME

ADDRESS

TELEPHONE

NAME

ADDRESS

TELEPHONE

NAME · Betty (Art Group)
ADDRESS (Doreen (Neswall)
TELEPHONE Margaret (Art Group)

NAME Marianne & Brian
ADDRESS Jerry
TELEPHONE Joan

NAME Pat & Arthur
ADDRESS Doreen R Bob
TELEPHONE Elaine (Art Group)

Joan Brooks
NAME Christine & Wally
ADDRESS Elaine MOGs
TELEPHONE Beryl "
Iris "

NAME Andrew & Christine McCarthy
ADDRESS Margaret Redditch
TELEPHONE Marian (Art Group)

NAME
ADDRESS Betty MOGs
Mary "
TELEPHONE Betty Withers

NAME Frank Turner
ADDRESS Derek (Art Group)
TELEPHONE Joan Fisher
Vera (MOGs

NAME Ann (Art Group)
ADDRESS Heather (Art Group)
TELEPHONE Sheila MOGs

Guy & Vera Potter
NAME Alma & Geoff
ADDRESS Margery
TELEPHONE Mary Maurice

NAME
ADDRESS Joyce & John Morgan
David Aldred
TELEPHONE

Joan & John Willcox
NAME Doreen McCarthy
ADDRESS Nigel & Christine
TELEPHONE Pauline & Dick Nichols

NAME Lilian Pike
ADDRESS Brenda & Steve Cooper
TELEPHONE Pam Thompson MOGs

ADDRESSES

Haydn & Jackie Dayhin

NAME Enid Mother
ADDRESS Terry Davis
TELEPHONE Brenda & Michael
Jean & John Knowles

NAME Ted Margi & family
Margaret Bellamy
TELEPHONE Christine & John W.

NAME Nora Groome (MOG's)
ADDRESS Jean Forman
David Singleton
TELEPHONE Ruth & George

NAME Janice & Simon & Raymond
ADDRESS John Barber
TELEPHONE Sheila Clifton

NAME Cousin Yvonne Ivy & Derek
ADDRESS Ken & Augie Pain
TELEPHONE Michael Oakley
Dottie

NAME Sylvia Garnett (MOG's)
ADDRESS Jean Lambert
TELEPHONE Christine & Terry

NAME Cousin June & Dave
ADDRESS Benson
Joan Murden
TELEPHONE Freda Belshaw
Linda & Adam

NAME June Cargill (MOG's)
ADDRESS
TELEPHONE Jean & Arthur
Gladys (Ryson)

NAME Graham & Rowena
ADDRESS Diana & family
TELEPHONE Susan Jack & Lucy

NAME Michael (Art Group)
ADDRESS Betty Deaton
TELEPHONE Andrew & Christine McCarthy
Milk man Paul

NAME Frank Boston
ADDRESS
TELEPHONE Audrey & Peter (Art Group)

NAME Caroline (Art Group)
ADDRESS Joan (Art Group)
Margaret Beebyer
TELEPHONE Jacky & Haydn

NAME wasn't Losiery it was lingerie

ADDRESS Howards because he [NAME] in charge of the factory
we assumed he owned it & of course he could have

TELEPHONE been managing it for [TELEPHONE] some one
Before he went standing market he worked for
NAME a Geoffrey McpherNAME in West Bridgford —

ADDRESS

My knowledge about George Pallant is almost nil.

TELEPHONE He was a cousin of the [TELEPHONE] Pinders & I think he lived
in Cinderhill at one [NAME] time & later in life he

ADDRESS belonged to the Bar [ADDRESS] Historic Society
By the way Florence didn't have any children. She

TELEPHONE adopted a young boy [TELEPHONE] unofficially.

NAME

ADDRESS

TELEPHONE

NAME

ADDRESS

TELEPHONE

NAME

ADDRESS

TELEPHONE

NAME

ADDRESS

TELEPHONE

NAME

ADDRESS

TELEPHONE

NAME

ADDRESS

TELEPHONE

Pleased to know you have recovered from a cold. You most likely
When the weather is so cold I hibernate ~ caught the germ from
Ethel or M<

NAME I have a photo which shows Blanche but I do not

ADDRESS have a photo of Florence. However I do believe

that Florence's married name was Cheetham

Blanche was named Burton ~ she had Two sons

called Albert & Ronald. His husband was Irish

& he went back to Ireland. According to my Mother

Blanche followed him to Ireland & gave birth to

three or

about four more children —

Wilfred is featured on Mother

& Dad's wedding photo

I can't tell you anything about my Grandpa on

Mother side of the family. He washed out on my

Mother & her three brothers when they were young

children

George was married to Sarah & they had Two

daughters Clara & Ivy.

Clara was still alive in 1982

Last week I obtained a copy of Mother & Dad's wedding photo for you

When I married my husband in 1946 he was a widower

with a son. He was Denis Charlton Oakley born in 1919.

Ken Prater definitely had a factory in Beeston

He manufactured ladies underwear & nightwear — it

ADDRESSES

NAME Joan

ADDRESS Mary & ~~Maurice~~

Christine & ~~Terry~~

~~Doreen~~, Bob, Carolyn

NAME Mary Oakland

ADDRESS Sheila Pike

Betty Marshall

TELEPHONE ~~Margaret Booty~~

Christine & Hetty

ADDRESS Cynthia

Freda

TELEPHONE Jack, Susan ~~Lucy~~

NAME Linda Adam & ~~Georgina~~

ADDRESS Christine & John

Janice & Raymond

TELEPHONE Guy & Partner

NAME ~~Margery & Bill~~

ADDRESS ~~Doreen McCarthy~~

~~Sylvia & Dorothy~~

TELEPHONE ~~Enid & Wesley~~

~~Iris Bott~~

NAME ~~Bernt Bertentos~~

ADDRESS ~~Margaret Robinson~~

~~Pam Thompson~~

TELEPHONE

June & ~~Dave~~

NAME Elaine Whitby

ADDRESS Margaret Bellamy

TELEPHONE ~~Beryl~~

Iris

NAME Ken & Angie

ADDRESS Sheila Clifford

Joan & Bernard Brooks

TELEPHONE ~~Ruth~~ & ~~George~~ Meacham

Margaret Reddish

NAME Betty Withers

ADDRESS Joan Fisher

TELEPHONE Joyce & ~~John~~ Morgan

NAME ~~Michael Steven~~

ADDRESS David Aldred

Brenda & Steve Cooper

TELEPHONE John Barber

Dottie Miller

ADDRESS Sylvia Garnett

~~Nora Crowne~~

TELEPHONE Mr & Mrs Miller

Terry Davie

Lucy & Ruhull

NAME

ADDRESS

David & Jodie

TELEPHONE